I COULD SING O ... JR
LOVE FOREVER

CONTENTS

— PIANO LEVEL —
LATE INTERMEDIATE/EARLY ADVANCED

ISBN 978-0-634-04827-2

HAL•LEONARD®
CORPORATION
7777 W. BLUEMOUND RD. P.O. BOX 13819 MILWAUKEE, WI 53213

Visit Hal Leonard Online at
www.halleonard.com

PREFACE

When I arranged a folio in this series called *Shout to the Lord!*, we could never have imagined the response it would illicit. Through numerous letters, e-mails and conversations, you let us know how much you appreciated the book and that more arrangements like this would be deeply appreciated. *I Could Sing of Your Love Forever* is an answer to your requests: additional pianistic settings of contemporary praise songs, in arrangements that will serve equally as well in a worship service or recital. In some cases, the song is dressed up harmonically or presented with variations. Sometimes it seemed best to just get out of the way and let a poignant melody spin out in a simple, straightforward manner.

It was truly a gift to live with these wonderful songs; working through each arrangement was a pleasure. I hope these settings will bless your music ministry.

Sincerely,
Phillip Keveren

BIOGRAPHY

Phillip Keveren, a multi-talented keyboard artist and composer, has composed original works in a variety of genres from piano solo to symphonic orchestra. Mr. Keveren gives frequent concerts and workshops for teachers and their students in the United States, Canada, Europe, and Asia. Mr. Keveren holds a B.M. in composition from California State University Northridge and a M.M. in composition from the University of Southern California.

AWESOME GOD

Words and Music by Rich Mullins

When He rolls up His sleeve, He ain't just "puttin' on the Ritz."
Our God is an awesome God!
There is thunder in His footsteps and lightnin' in His fist.
Our God is an awesome God!

And the Lord wasn't jokin' when He kicked 'em out of Eden;
It wasn't for no reason that He shed His blood.
His return is very close and so you better be believin'
That our God is an awesome God!

CHORUS:
Our God is an awesome God;
He reigns from heaven above.
With wisdom, pow'r and love,
Our God is an awesome God!

CHORUS

And when the sky was starless
In the void of the night,
Our God is an awesome God!
He spoke into the darkness
And created the light.
Our God is an awesome God!

The judgment and wrath He poured out on Sodom,
The mercy and grace He gave us at the cross.
I hope that we have not too quickly forgotten
That our God is an awesome God!

CHORUS

Our God is an awesome God!
Our God is an awesome God!

This song is a contemporary classic. It has proven to be a longstanding favorite in my church. The musical material lends itself well to a theme and variation treatment, and this setting explores the dramatic possibilities inherent in the theme. This arrangement would work in a concert setting as well as in a worship environment.

PK

AWESOME GOD

Words and Music by RICH MULLINS
Arranged by Phillip Keveren

Boldly (♩ = 140)

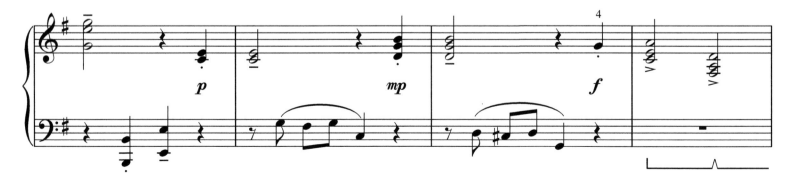

Slightly faster

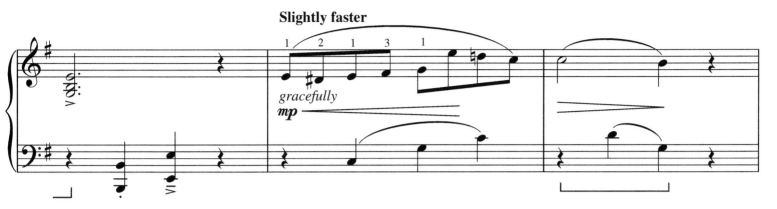

gracefully

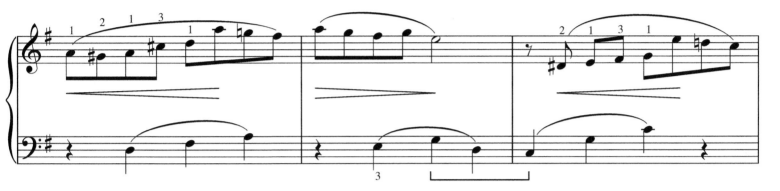

Triumphantly (♩ = 118)

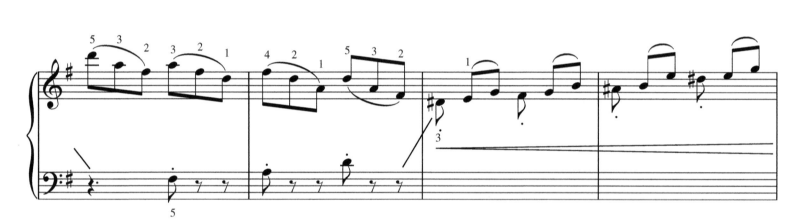

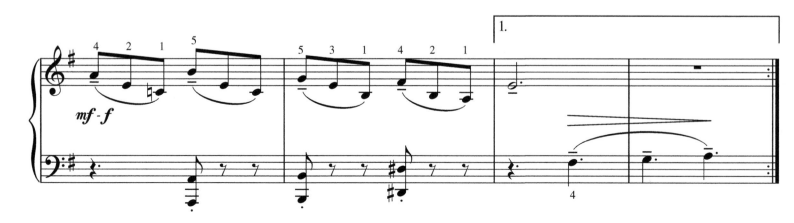

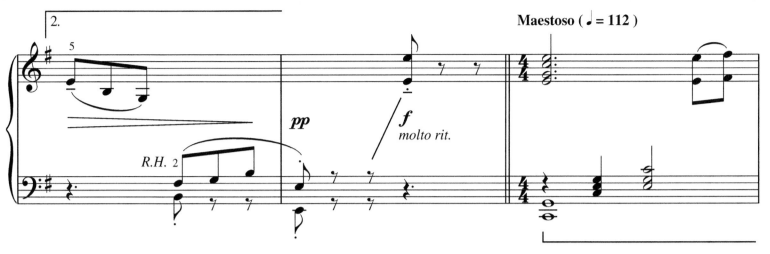

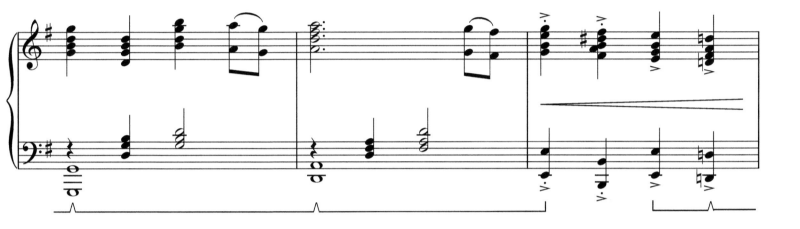

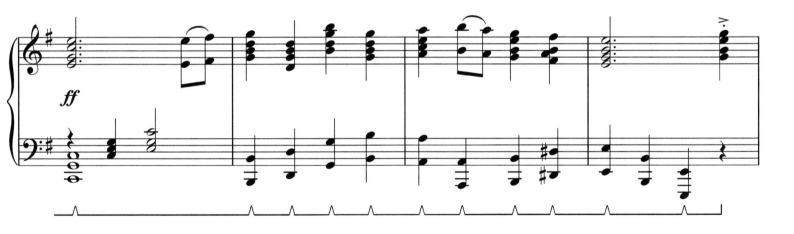

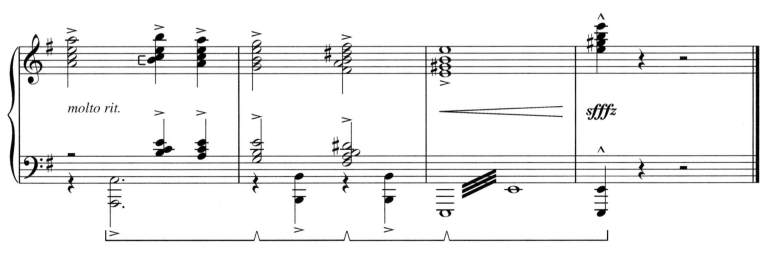

THE HEART OF WORSHIP

Words and Music by Matt Redman

When the music fades, all is stripped away, and I simply come,
Longing just to bring something that's of worth that will bless Your heart.

CHORUS:
I'll bring You more than a song,
For a song in itself is not what You have required.
You search much deeper within
Through the way things appear;
You're looking into my heart.
I'm coming back to the heart of worhip,
And it's all about You, all about You, Jesus.
I'm sorry, Lord, for the thing I've made it,
When it's all about You, all about You, Jesus.

King of endless worth, no one could express how much You deserve.
Though I'm weak and poor, all I have is Yours, ev'ry single breath.

CHORUS

I was immediately drawn to this lyrical song. It has come to mean a great deal to my congregation. Play it freely, allowing the melody to sing in an unhurried manner.

PK

THE HEART OF WORSHIP

Words and Music by MATT REDMAN
Arranged by Phillip Keveren

Slowly, tenderly (♩ = 76)

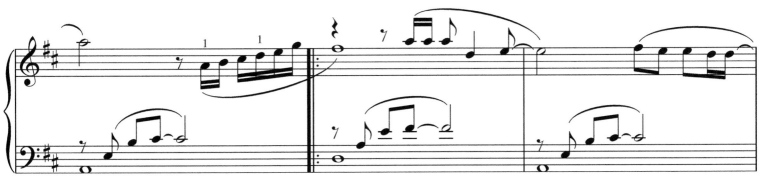

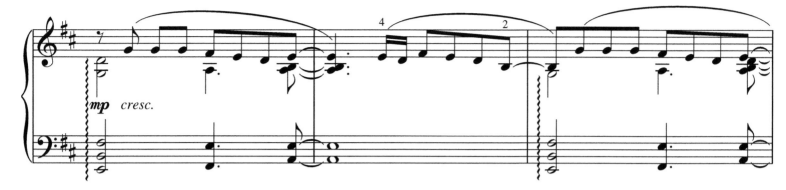

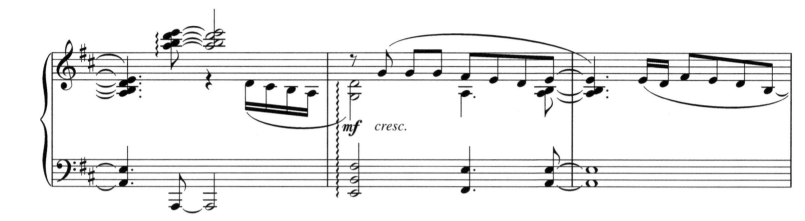

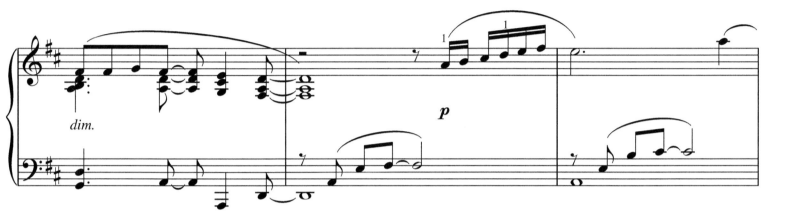

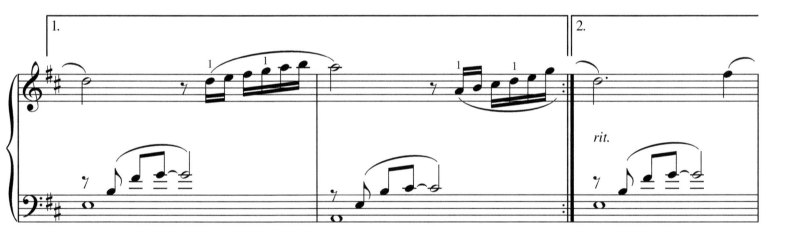

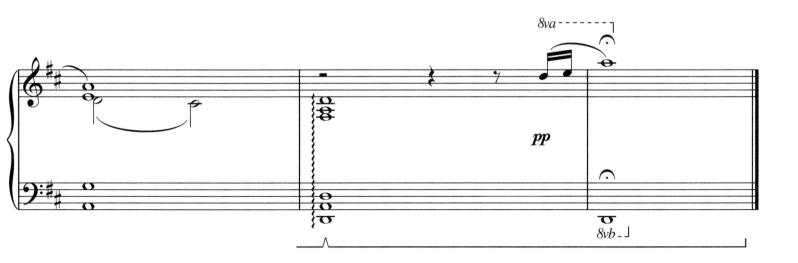

HOLY GROUND

Words and Music by Geron Davis

As I walked through the door I sensed His presence,
And I knew this was a place where love abounds.
For this is the temple, Jehovah God abides here,
And we are standing in His presence on holy ground.

CHORUS:
We are standing on holy ground,
And I know that there are angels all around.
Let us praise Jesus now.
We are standing in His presence on holy ground.

In His presence there is joy beyond measure,
And at His feet peace of mind can still be found.
If you have a need, I know He has the answer.
Reach out and claim it, you are standing on holy ground.

CHORUS

Let us praise Jesus now.
We are standing in His presence,
We are standing in His presence,
We are standing in His presence on holy ground.

I first heard this powerful song in my younger brother's wedding. It was an emotional performance that I'll always remember. I immediately looked for the sheet music and began to use it in worship services. I really enjoyed working on a pianistic arrangement of this wonderful composition.

PK

HOLY GROUND

Words and Music by GERON DAVIS
Arranged by Phillip Keveren

Reverently (♩ = 78-82)

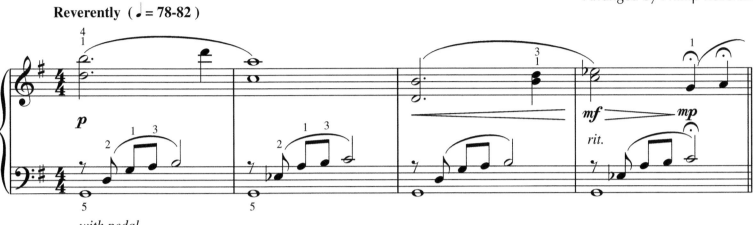

with pedal

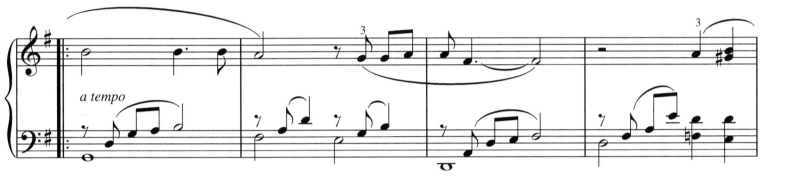

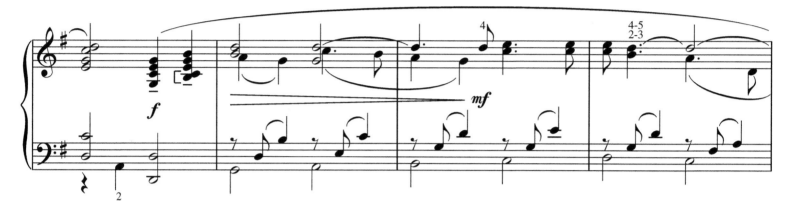

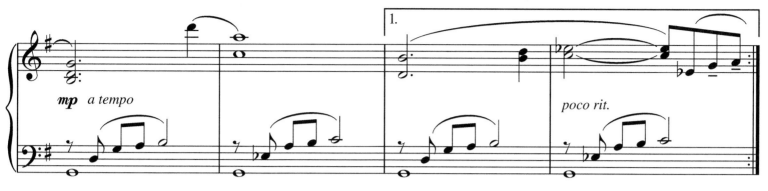

Slower, with majesty

I COULD SING OF YOUR LOVE FOREVER

Words and Music by Martin Smith

Over the mountains and the sea
Your river runs with love for me,
And I will open up my heart
And let the Healer set me free.
I'm happy to be in the truth
And I will daily lift my hands,
For I will always sing of when Your love came down.
I could sing, I could sing of Your love forever.

I could sing of Your love forever,
I could sing of Your love forever,
Etc.

Oh, I feel like dancing;
It's foolishness, I know.
But when the world has seen the light
They will dance with joy like we're dancing now.

I could sing of Your love forever,
I could sing of Your love forever,
Etc.

This melody has a way of sticking with you. Even though it is repetitive, it has an attractive quality that is undeniable. This arrangement should be played in a flowing, impressionistic style. I believe it would make an effective offertory solo.

PK

I COULD SING OF YOUR LOVE FOREVER

Words and Music by MARTIN SMITH
Arranged by Phillip Keveren

Rubato, with wonder

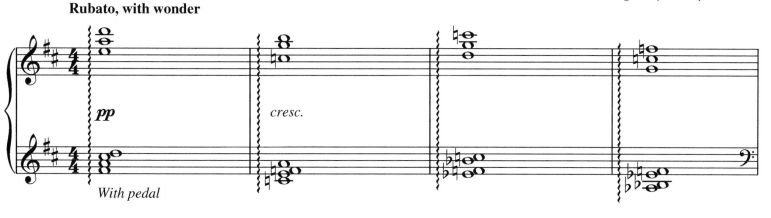

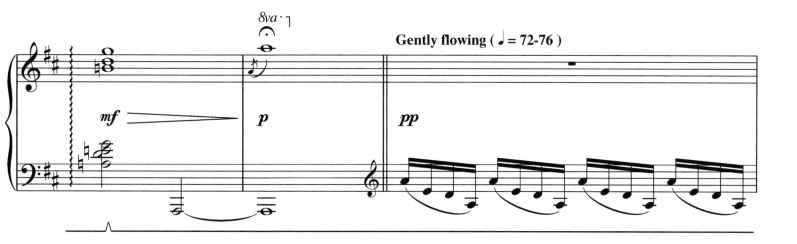

Gently flowing (♩ = 72-76)

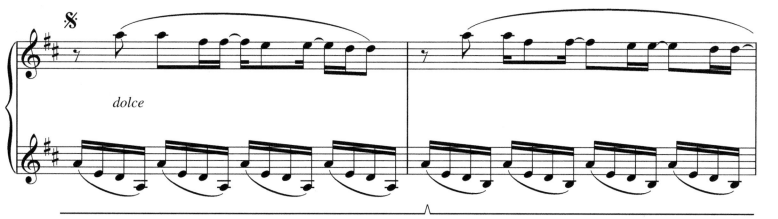

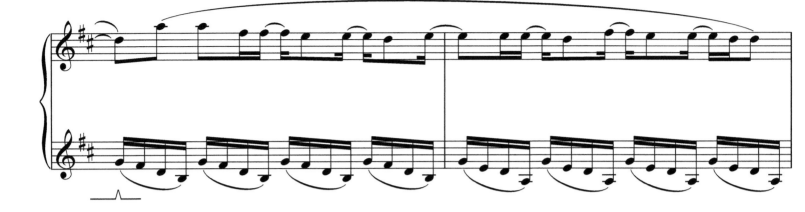

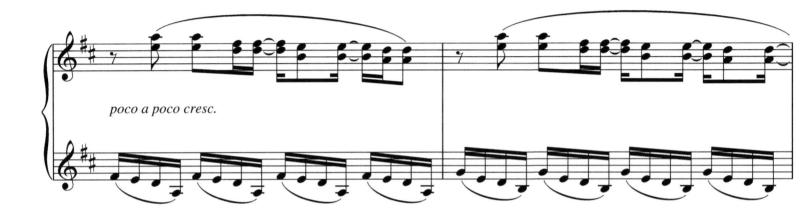

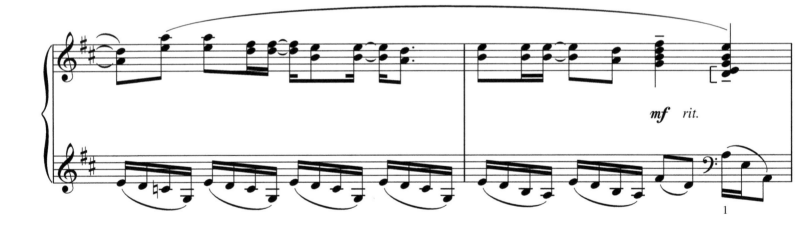

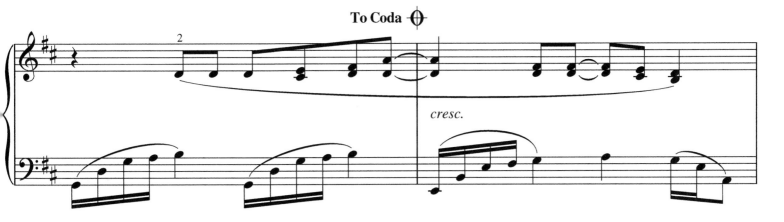

CODA

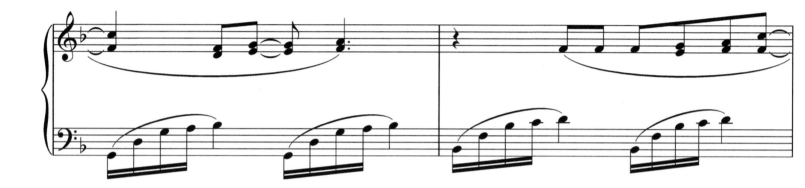

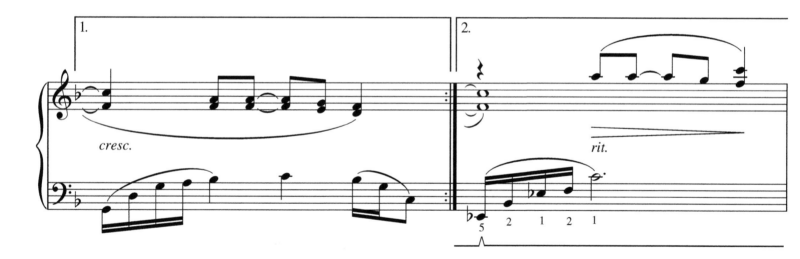

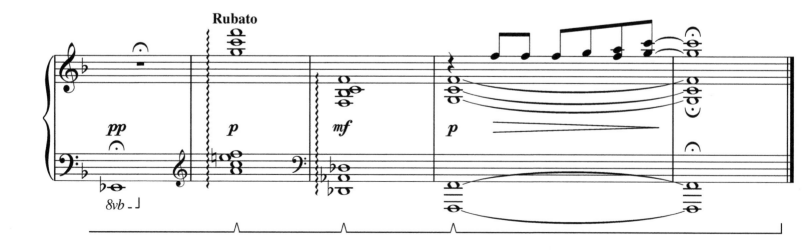

IN THIS VERY ROOM

Words and Music by Ron and Carol Harris

In this very room there's quite enough love for one like me,
And in this very room there's quite enough joy for one like me.
And there's quite enough hope and quite enough power to chase away any gloom,
For Jesus, Lord Jesus is in this very room.

And in this very room there's quite enough love for all of us,
And in this very room there's quite enough joy for all of us.
And there's quite enough hope and quite enough power to chase away any gloom,
For Jesus, Lord Jesus is in this very room.

And in this very room there's quite enough love for all the world,
And in this very room there's quite enough joy for all the world.
And there's quite enough hope and quite enough power to chase away any gloom,
For Jesus, Lord Jesus is in this very room.

Ron and Carol Harris, the writers of this superb song, are dear friends of mine. I am deeply grateful to Ron for giving me the opportunity to write for his publishing company many years ago, one of the breaks that started my career as an arranger and composer. This song has become one of the most beloved praise songs in the church today. It is a magical blending of words and music, and I hope this arrangement serves it well.

PK

IN THIS VERY ROOM

Words and Music by RON HARRIS
and CAROL HARRIS
Arranged by Phillip Keveren

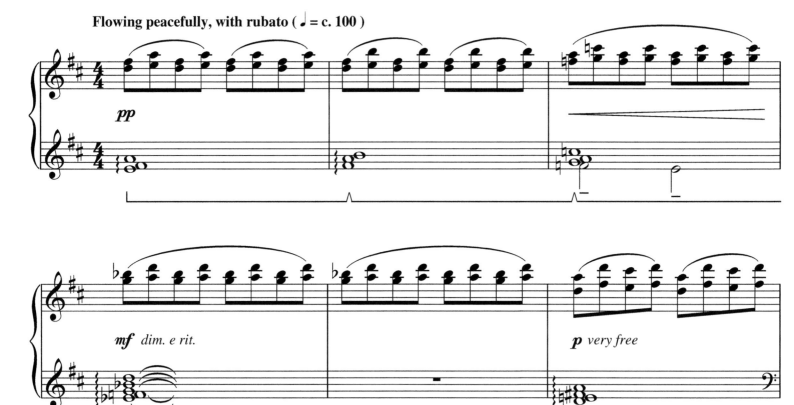

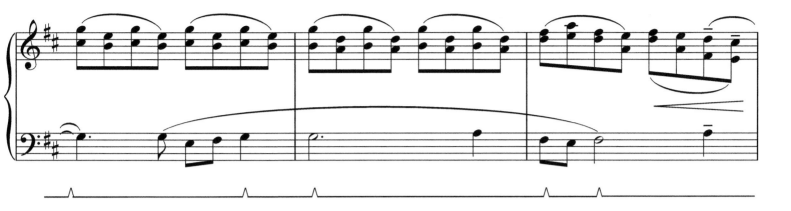

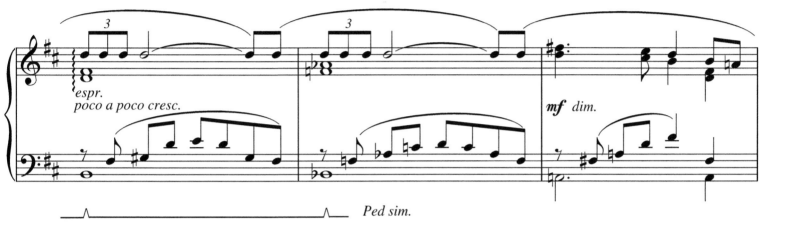

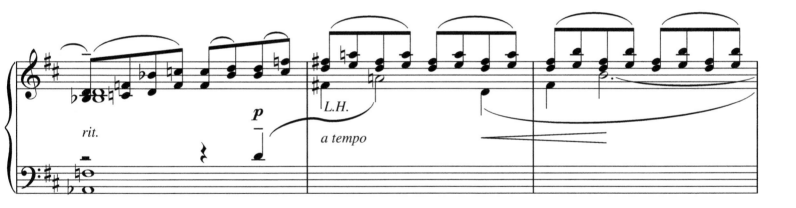

With grandeur (♩ = 88)

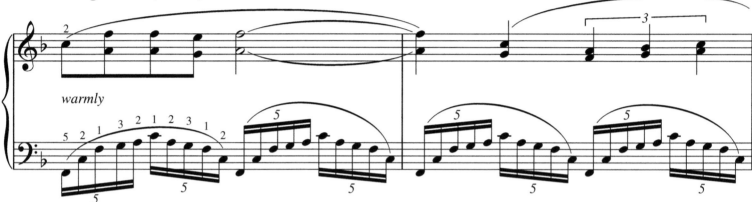

warmly

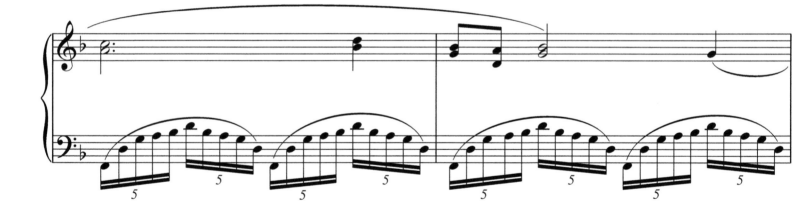

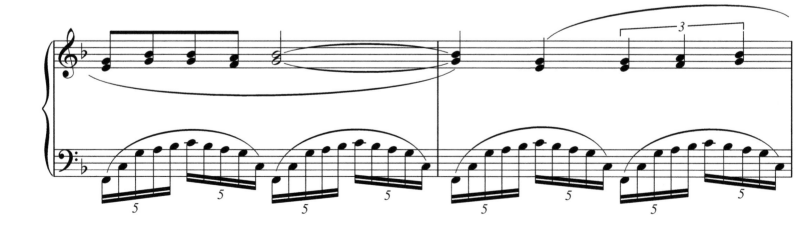

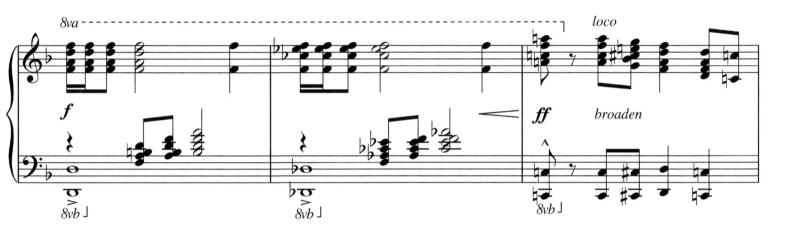

Slowly, reflectively

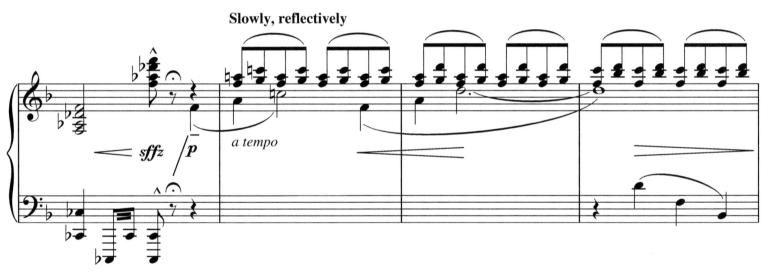

I LOVE YOU LORD

Words and Music by Laurie Klein

I love You, Lord, and I lift my voice
To worship You. O my soul, rejoice!
Take joy, my King, in what you hear.
May it be a sweet, sweet sound in Your ear.

This praise song is so well known that I feel it can withstand a little harmonic variation. Some subtle shadings bring the melody into a slightly different light. Play it spaciously and with deep expression.

PK

I LOVE YOU LORD

Words and Music by LAURIE KLEIN
Arranged by Phillip Keveren

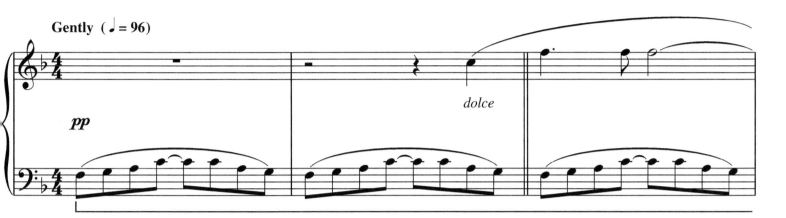

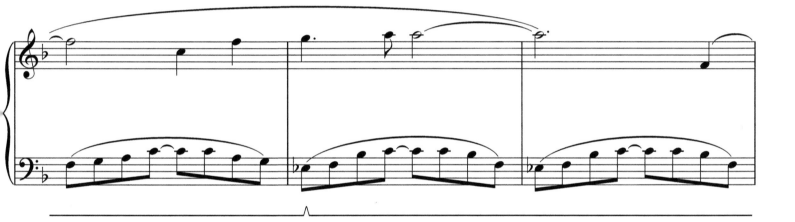

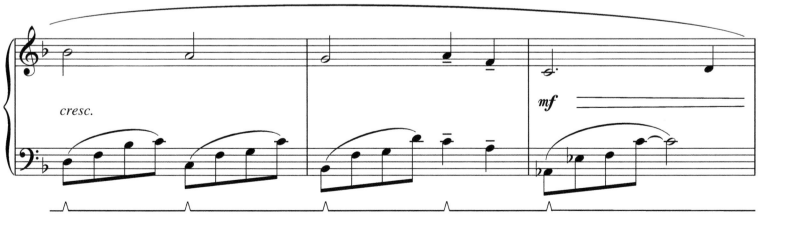

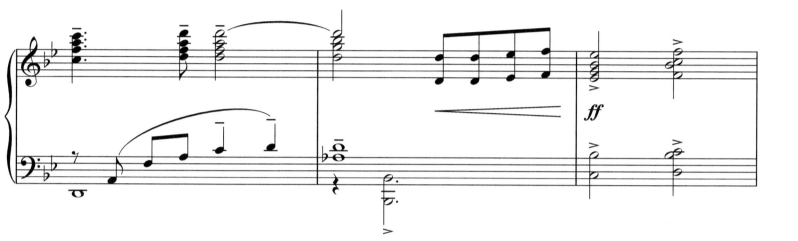

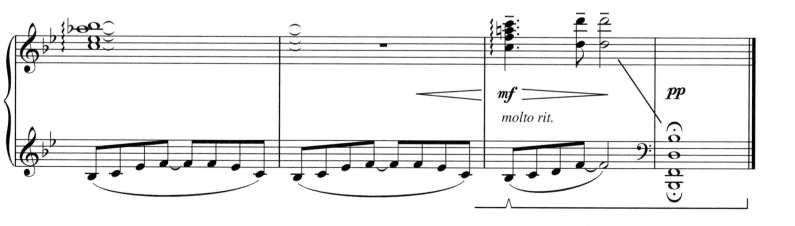

KNOWING YOU (ALL I ONCE HELD DEAR)

Words and Music by Graham Kendrick

All I once held dear, built my life upon,
All this world reveres and wars to own.
All I once thought gain I have counted loss,
Spent and worthless now compared to this.

CHORUS:
Knowing You, Jesus,
Knowing You, there is no greater thing.
You're my all, You're the best,
You're my joy, my righteousness,
And I love You, Lord.

Now my heart's desire is to know You more,
To be found in You, and known as Yours.
To possess by faith what I could not earn,
All surpassing gift of righteousness.

CHORUS

Oh, to know the pow'r of Your risen life
And to know You in Your sufferings.
To become like You in Your death, my Lord,
So with You to live and never die.

CHORUS

This is a very moving melody that sings beautifully on the piano. Take your time with the arrangement, allowing the phrasing to spin out in a rubato manner. Voice the full chords carefully so that the melody rises above the colorful harmonics.

PK

KNOWING YOU
(All I Once Held Dear)

Words and Music by GRAHAM KENDRICK
Arranged by Phillip Keveren

Rubato, thoughtfully (♩ = c. 60)

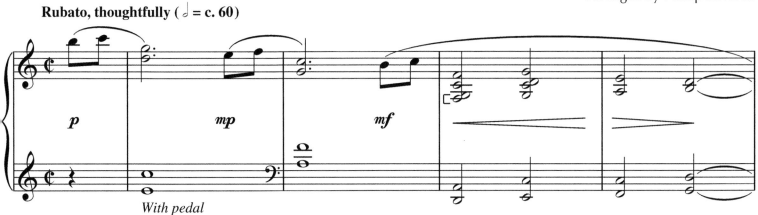

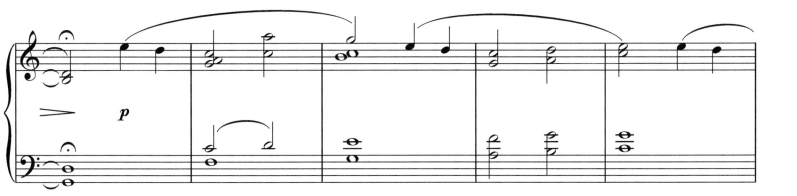

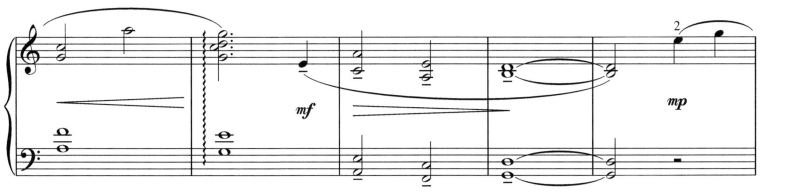

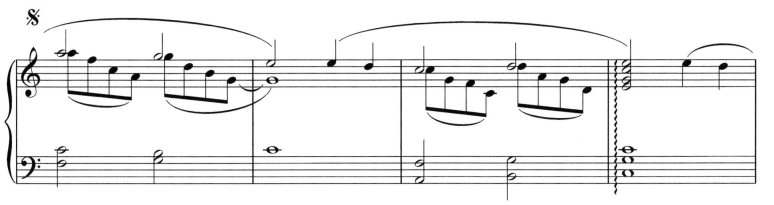

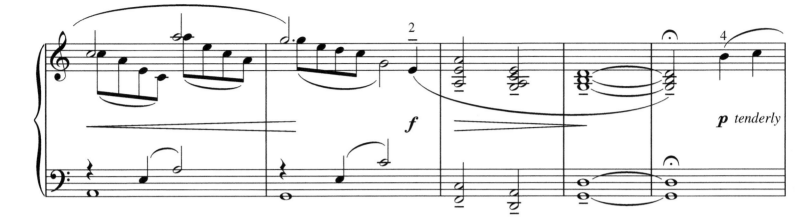

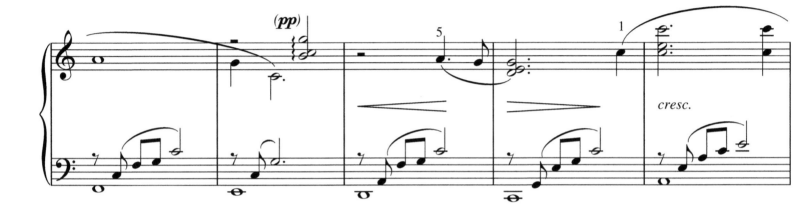

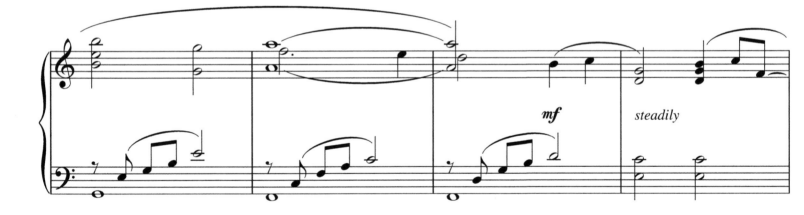

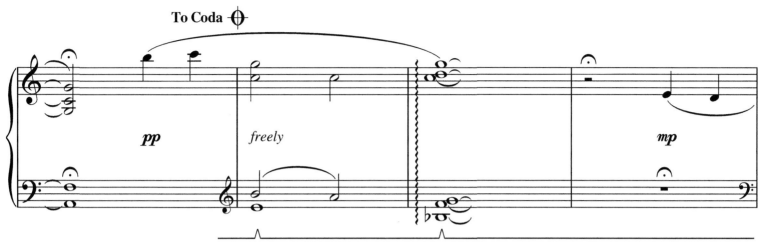

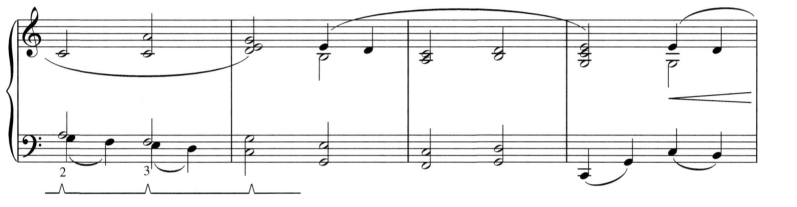

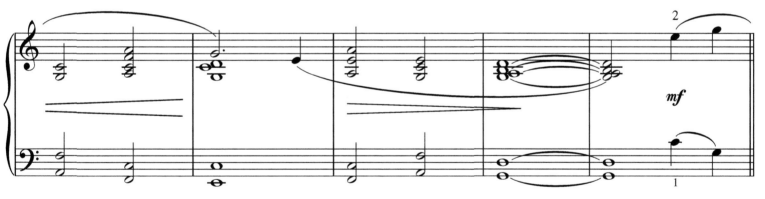

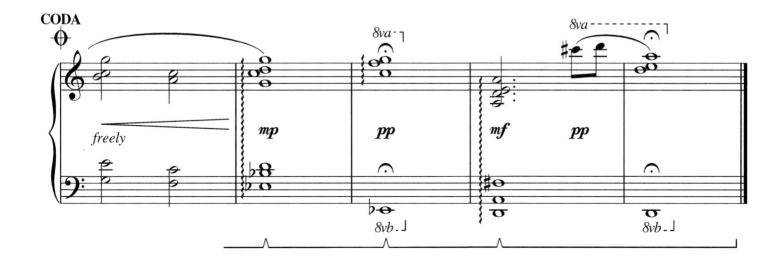

LET MY WORDS BE FEW
(I'LL STAND IN AWE OF YOU)

Words and Music by Matt Redman and Beth Redman

You are God in heaven,
And here I am on earth.
So I'll let my words be few.
Jesus, I am so in love with You.
And I'll stand in awe of You.
Yes, I'll stand in awe of You.
And I'll let my words be few.
Jesus, I am so in love with you.

The simplest of all love songs
I want to bring to You.
So I'll let my words be few.
Jesus, I am so in love with You.
And I'll stand in awe of You.
Yes, I'll stand in awe of You.
And I'll let my words be few.
Jesus, I am so in love with you.

So I'll stand, and I'll stand in awe of You.
Jesus, yes, I'll stand in awe of You.
The more we see the more we love.
And I'll stand in awe of You.
I'll stand in awe of You.
And I'll let my word be few.
Jesus, I am so in love with You.

I was introduced to this song through my daughter's youth group. It has a simple, yet touching melody. A direct, unadorned performance of this arrangement will be the most effective.

PK

LET MY WORDS BE FEW
(I'll Stand in Awe of You)

Words and Music by MATT REDMAN
and BETH REDMAN
Arranged by Phillip Keveren

Quietly (♩ = 86)

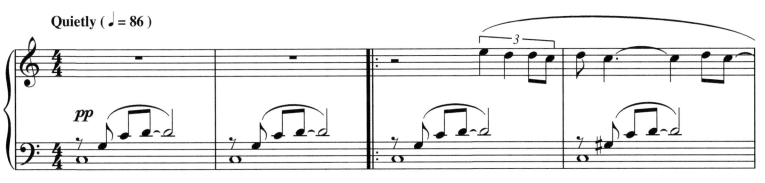

With pedal

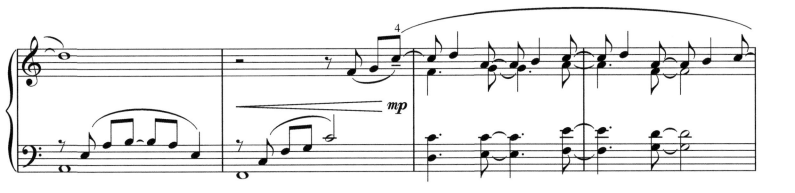

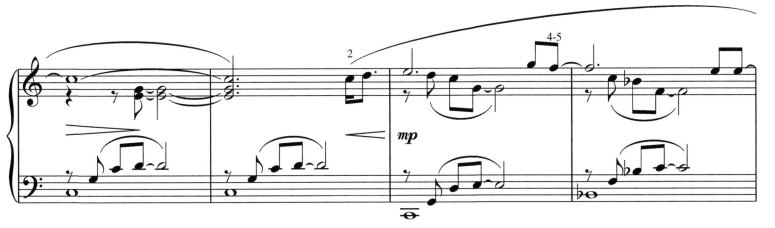

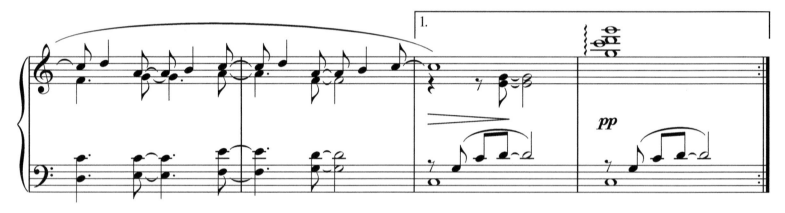

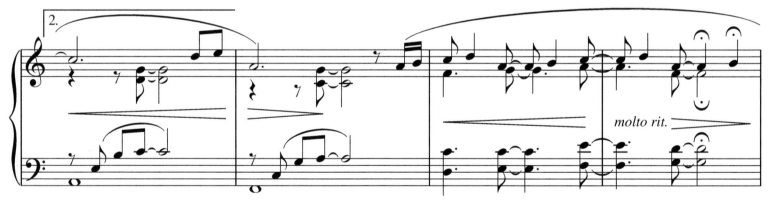

MOVE IN ME

Words by Wayne Kirkpatrick
Music by Michael W. Smith

I am only human, struggling to find
Confidence in all that I believe.
You are only holy, You are love divine.
And You have said to ask and I'll receive.

So I have come to pray that You will come and feed
The hunger here inside me to grow stronger in the faith.
There's a longing and a need to have You ever closer.
Come fill me.

'Cause when You move in me it's like a symphony,
A timeless melody that soothes my soul.
Though silent, I can tell that You're alive and well.
'Cause I can feel You move in me.

What they try to tell me is that Your love is false,
And faith is just a way I chose to feel.
And that there was no meaning to You upon the cross,
And I should reach for something that is real.

And when those words are said, the questions in me start,
And I don't have any answers until I stop thinking with my head
And start list'ning to my heart. And there I find my assurance.
I tell them

That when You move in me it's like a symphony,
A timeless melody that soothes my soul.
Though silent, I can tell that You're alive and well.
'Cause I can feel You move in me.

Michael W. Smith is one of the most gifted melody writers working in Contemporary Christian music. His compositions are always so well crafted, and as a result, a joy to arrange. This song is no exception, with a melody that sings, a rich harmonic progression, and a syncopated feel that gives it a distinct character.

PK

MOVE IN ME

Words and Music by MICHAEL W. SMITH
and WAYNE KIRKPATRICK
Arranged by Phillip Keveren

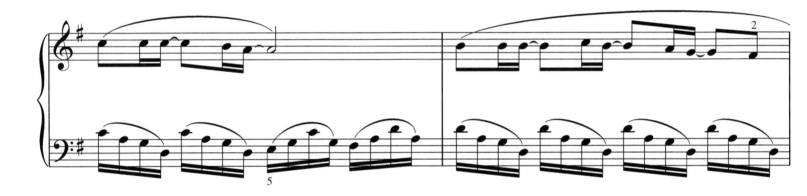

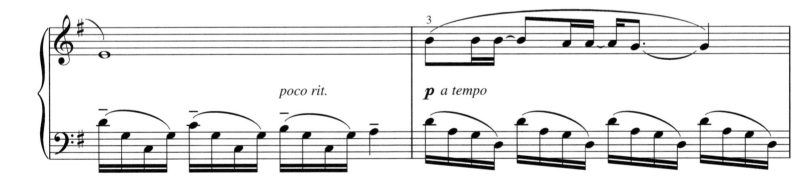

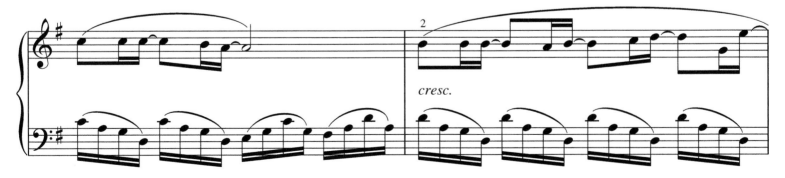

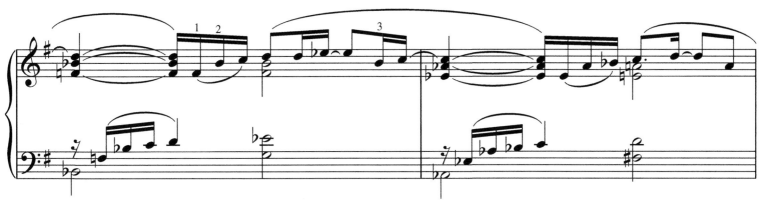

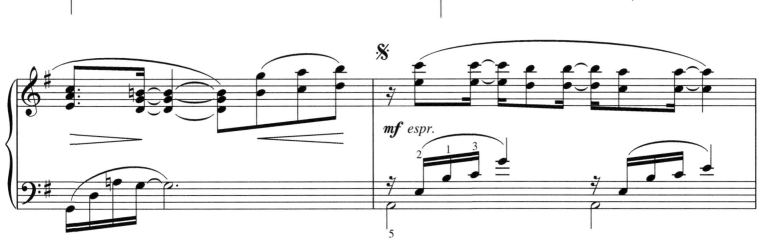

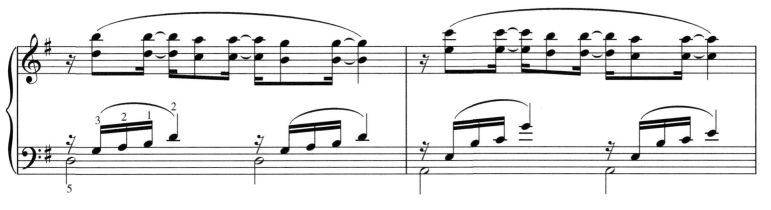

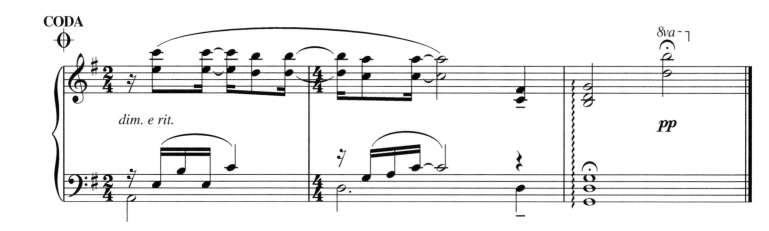

THE POWER OF YOUR LOVE

Words and Music by Geoff Bullock

Lord, I come to You,
Let my heart be changed, renewed,
Flowing from the grace that I've found in You.

And Lord, I've come to know
The weakness I see in me will be stripped away
By the power of Your love.

CHORUS:
Hold me close, let Your love surround me;
Bring me near, draw me to Your side.
And as I wait, I'll rise up like the eagle
And I will soar with You
Your spirit leads me on in the pow'r of Your love.

Lord, unveil my eyes,
Let me see You face to face,
The knowledge of Your love as You live in me.

Lord, renew my mind,
As your will unfolds in my life, in living ev'ryday
In the pow'r of Your love.

CHORUS

A beautiful piece with a strong melody, this composition makes a very dramatic musical statement. I think this is one of the finest songs in contemporary praise music.

PK

THE POWER OF YOUR LOVE

Words and Music by GEOFF BULLOCK
Arranged by Phillip Keveren

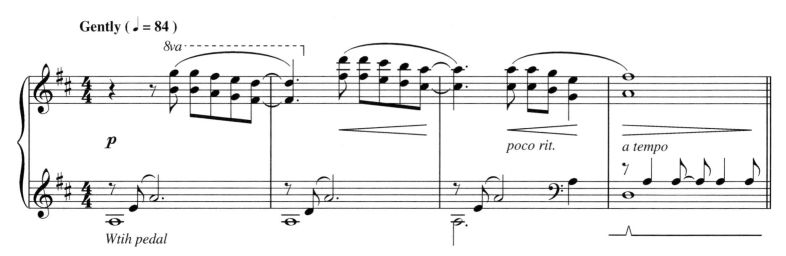

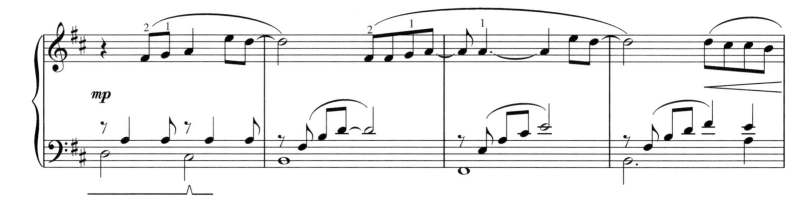

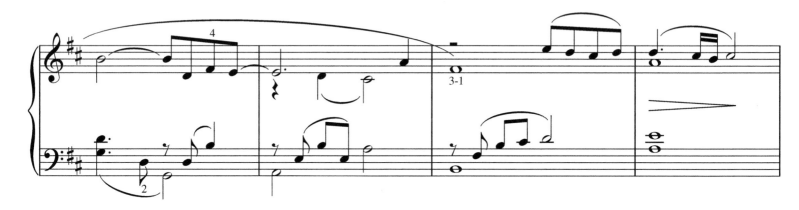

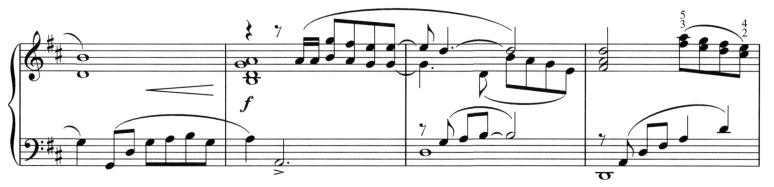

Slowly, stately

MY UTMOST FOR HIS HIGHEST

Words and Music by Twila Paris

When the Savior came to earth,
Answer to the endless fall,
He became a man by birth
Then He died to save us all.

May we never come to Him
With half a heart.
All that He deserves is nothing less
Than all I am and all you are.

CHORUS:
For His highest, I give my utmost.
To the King of Kings, to the Lord of Hosts,
For His glory, for His goodness,
I will give my utmost for His highest.

Standing in this holy place,
Let us all remember here,
Covered only by His grace,
We are bought with blood so dear.

May we never bring with lesser offering,
He alone is worthy to receive
The life we live,
The song we sing.

CHORUS

Any dream that tries
To turn my heart will be denied.
Anything at all that weighs me down
I will gladly cast aside.

CHORUS

This song builds from a gentle verse into a powerful chorus. Make the most of the dynamic contrasts. I think you will achieve the best reading of this arrangement if you study the lyric, allowing it to inform your phrasing.

PK

MY UTMOST FOR HIS HIGHEST

Words and Music by TWILA PARIS
Arranged by Phillip Keveren

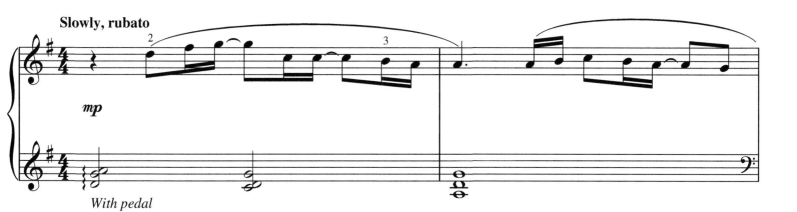

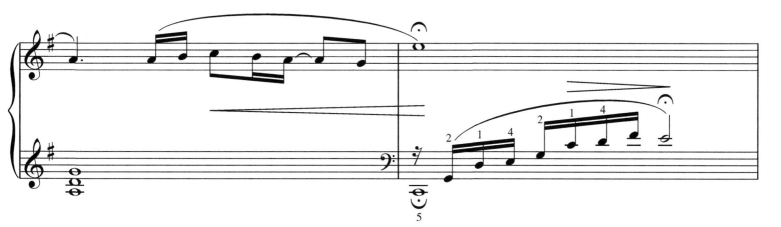

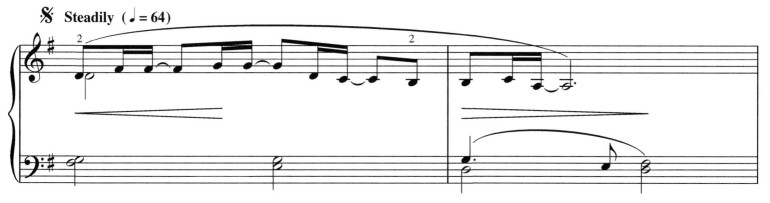

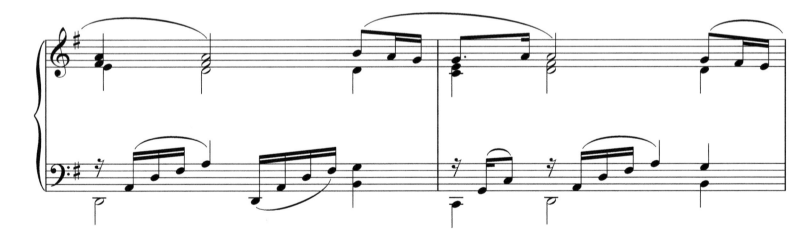

OPEN THE EYES OF MY HEART

Words and Music by Paul Baloche

Open the eyes of my heart, Lord.
Open the eyes of my heart.
I want to see You.
I want to see You.
Open the eyes of my heart, Lord.
Open the eyes of my heart.
I want to see You.
I want to see You,
To see You high and lifted up,
Shining in the light of Your glory.
Pour out Your power and love
As we sing holy, holy, holy.

To see You high and lifted up,
Shining in the light of Your glory.
Pour out Your power and love
As we sing holy, holy, holy.

This arrangement needs to be played with a strong rhythmic sense, maintaining a steady pulse in both the piano and forte passages. Although the song is typically heard with a pop rhythm section underpinning, it is fun to place it in a pianistic setting, using "classical" arranging devices to move it forward.

PK

OPEN THE EYES OF MY HEART

Words and Music by PAUL BALOCHE
Arranged by Phillip Keveren

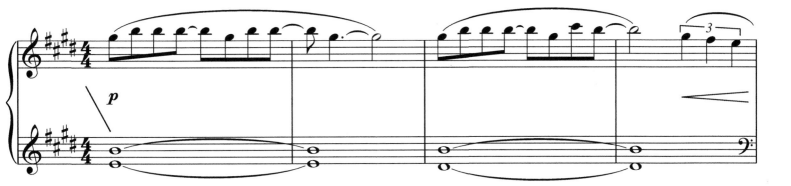

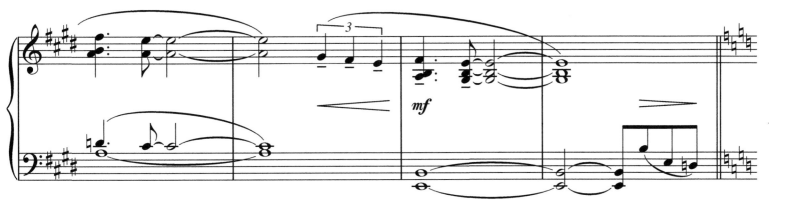

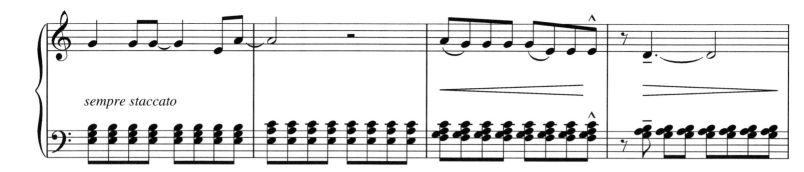

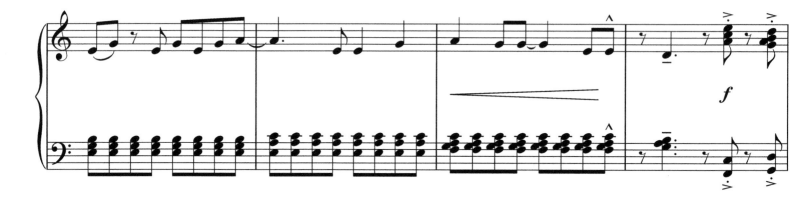

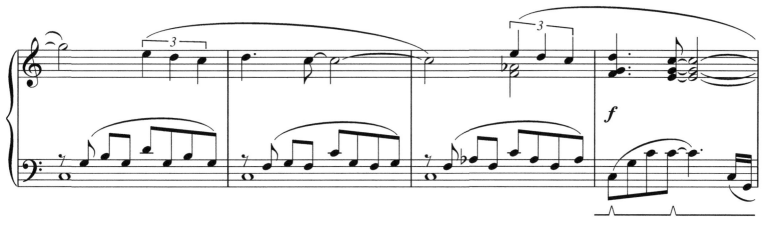

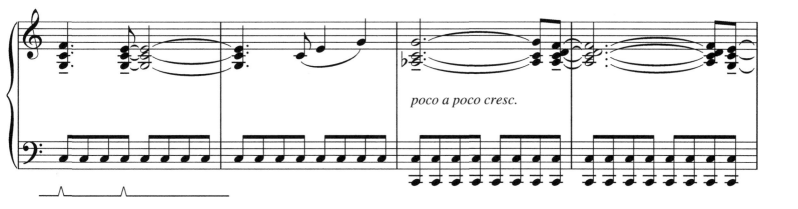

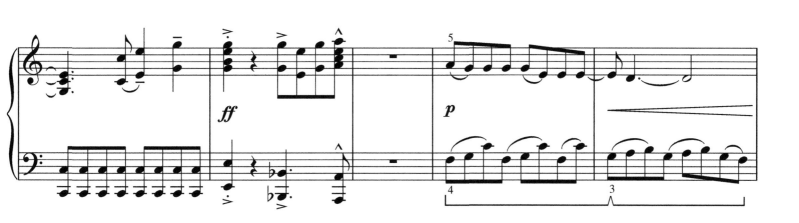

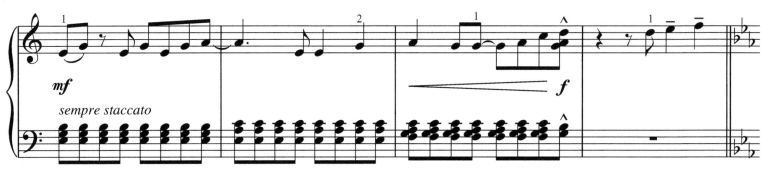

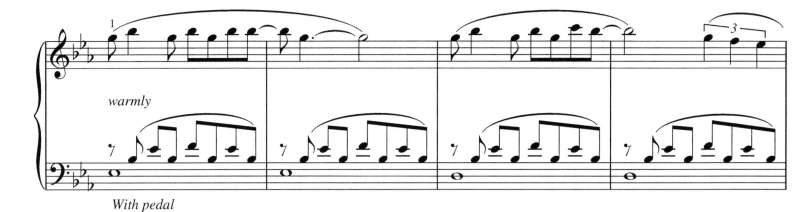

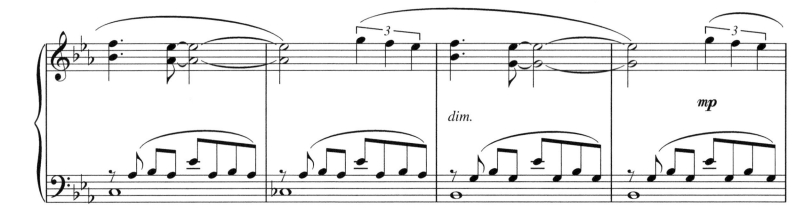

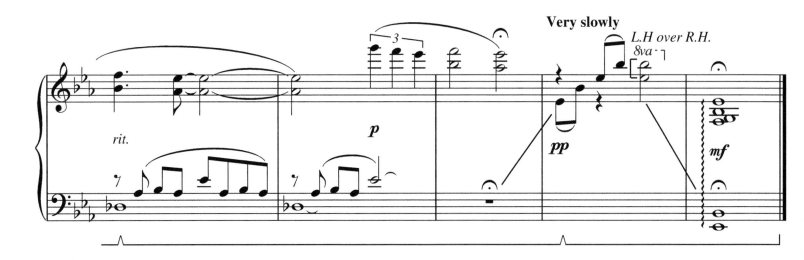

THERE IS A REDEEMER

Words and Music by Melody Green

VERSE 1:
There is a redeemer,
Jesus, God's own Son.
Precious Lamb of God, Messiah,
Holy One.

Jesus, my redeemer,
Name above all names.
Precious Lamb of God, Messiah,
Oh for sinners slain.

CHORUS:
Thank You, oh my Father,
For giving us Your Son,
And leaving Your spirit
Till the work on earth is done.

When I stand in glory,
I will see His face,
And there I'll serve my King forever
In that holy place.

CHORUS

VERSE 1

CHORUS

And leaving Your spirit till the work on earth is done.

What a wonderful composition this is! It has always had a timeless quality to me, sounding like a rich, traditional hymn, yet somehow contemporary as well. I may have spent more time on this arrangement than any other in the collection, trying to get just the right take on it. Play it slowly and expressively.

PK

THERE IS A REDEEMER

Words and Music by MELODY GREEN
Arranged by Phillip Keveren

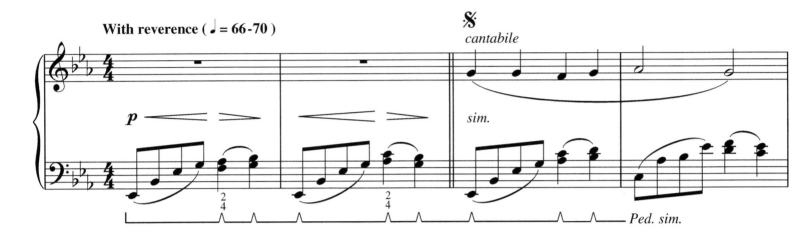

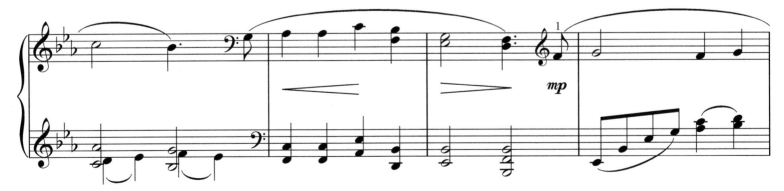

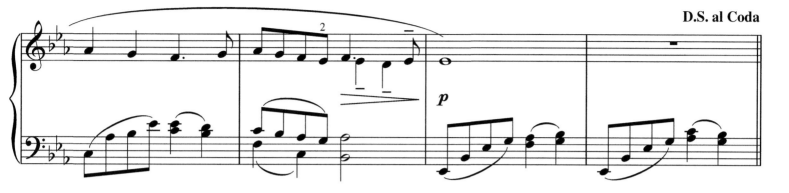

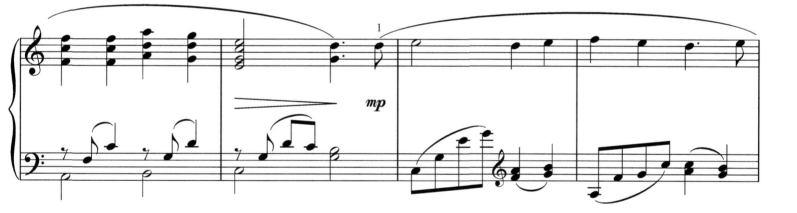

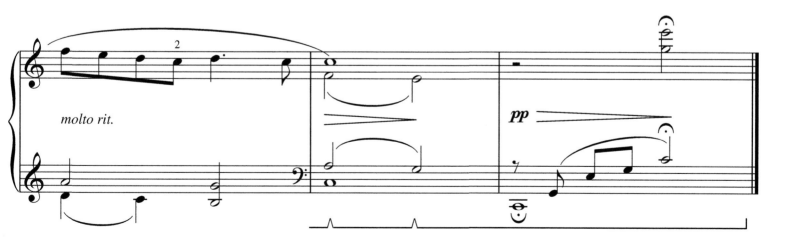

SHOUT TO THE NORTH

Words and Music by Martin Smith

Men of faith, rise up and sing
Of the great and glorious King.
You are strong when you feel weak;
In your brokenness, complete.

CHORUS 1:
Shout to the north and the south;
Sing to the east and the west.
Jesus is Savior to all,
Lord of heaven and earth.

Rise up, women of the truth;
Stand and sing to broken hearts.
Who can know the healing pow'r
Of our awesome King of love?

CHORUS 1

CHORUS 2:
We will shout to the north and the south,
Sing to the east and the west.
Jesus is Savior to all,
Lord of heaven and earth.

We've been through fire,
We've been through rain,
We've been refined by the pow'r of His name.
We've fallen deeper in love with You;
You've burned the truth on our lips.

CHORUS 2

Rise up, church, with broken wings;
Fill this place with songs again,
Of our God who reigns on high.
By His grace, again we'll fly.

CHORUS 1

CHORUS 2

Play this piece with unrelenting rhythmic drive, much like an Irish jig. This setting would be effective as a worship service postlude.

PK

SHOUT TO THE NORTH

Words and Music by MARTIN SMITH
Arranged by Phillip Keveren

With driving energy (♩. = 64)

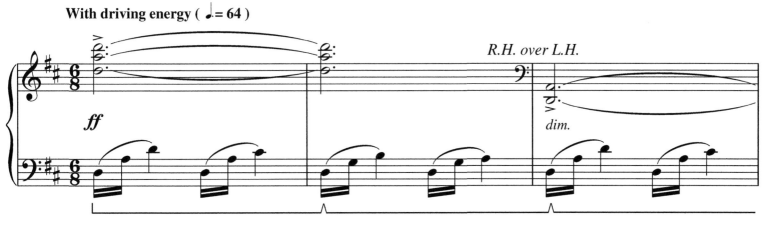

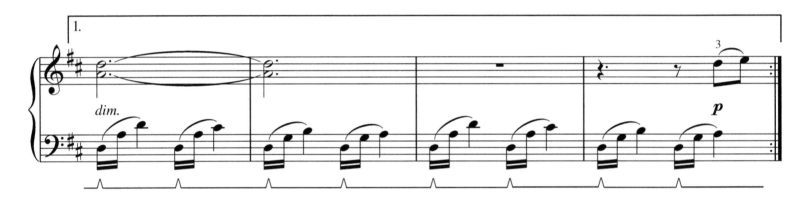

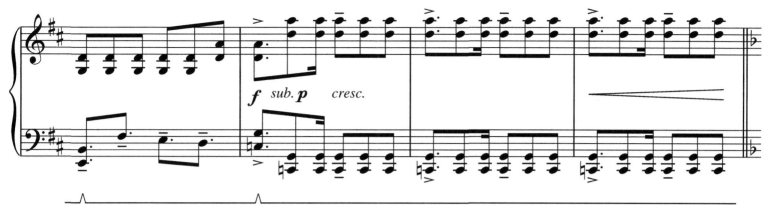

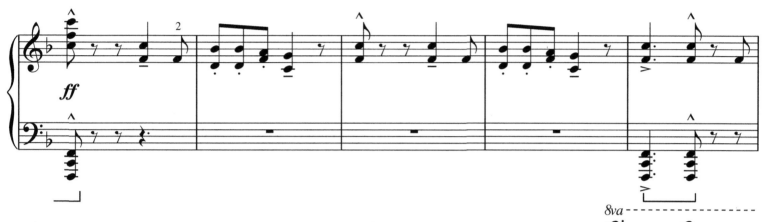

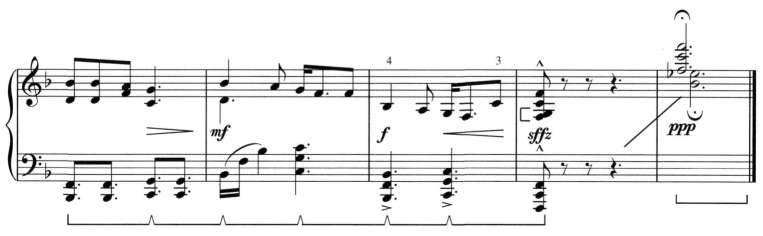

THE POTTER'S HAND

Words and Music by Darlene Zschech

Beautiful Lord, wonderful Savior,
I know for sure all of my days are held in Your hand,
Crafted into Your perfect plan.

You gently call me into Your presence,
Guiding me by Your Holy Spirit;
Teach me, dear Lord, to live all of my life through Your eyes.

I'm captured by Your holy calling,
Set me apart, I know You're drawing
Me to Yourself; lead me, Lord, I pray.

Take me, mold me, use me, fill me,
I give my life to the Potter's hand.
Call me, guide me, lead me, walk beside me;
I give my life to the Potter's hand.

This song comes from the same composer who penned "Shout to the Lord." It works well as a piano solo. The composition builds gradually, allowing for a full range of expression.

PK

THE POTTER'S HAND

Words and Music by DARLENE ZSCHECH
Arranged by Phillip Keveren

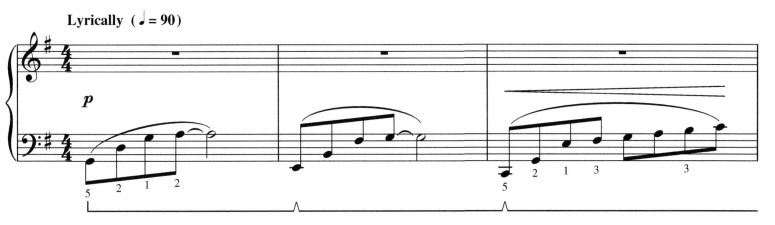

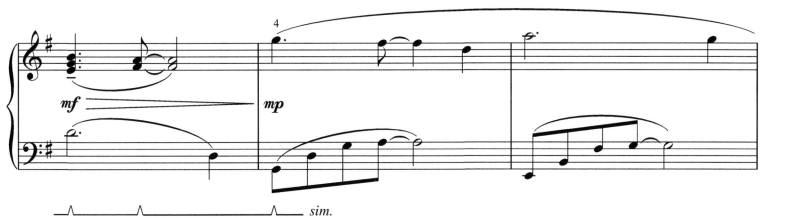

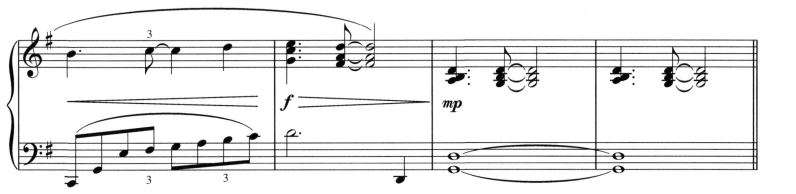

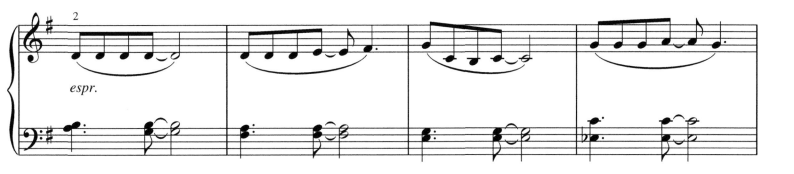

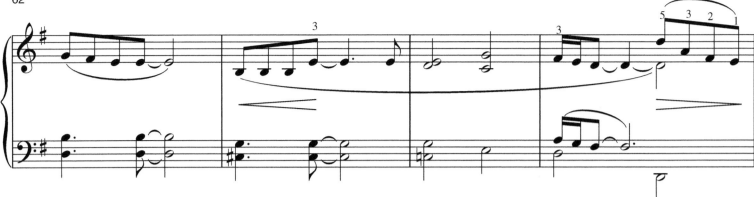

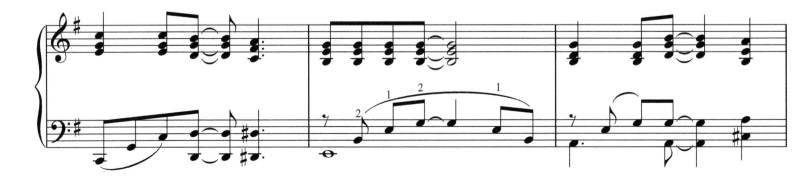

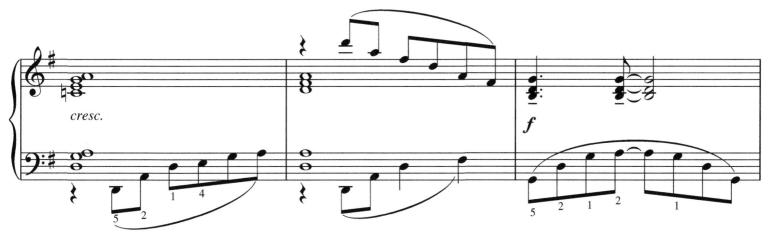

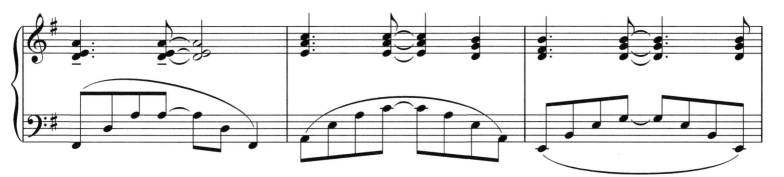

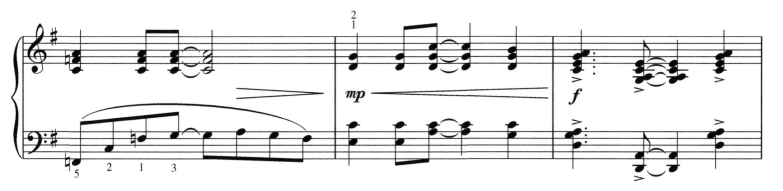

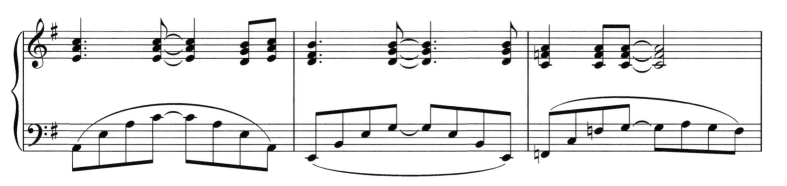

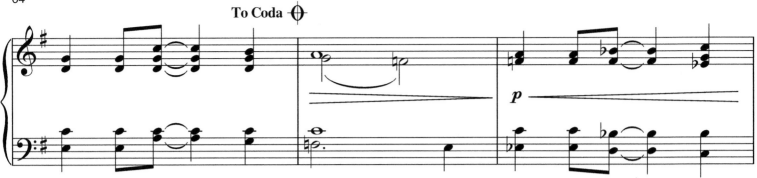

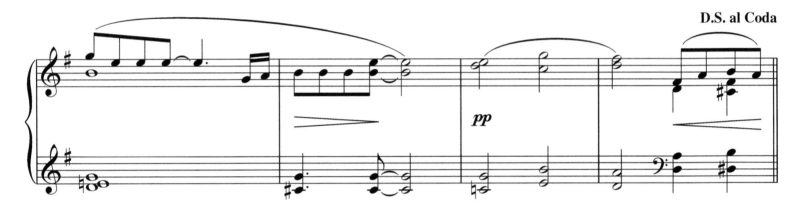

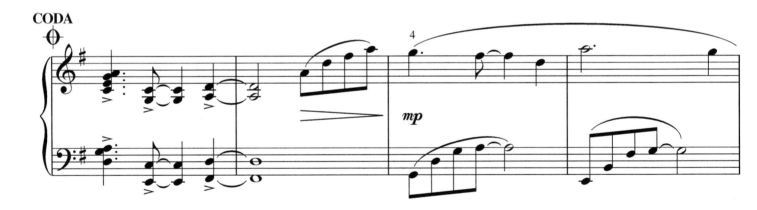